KEEP KEEP KEEP KEE
CALM CALM CALM CALM
AND AND AND AND
PRAY PRAY PRAY PRAY

KEEP KEEP KEEP
CALM CALM CALM
AND AND AND
PRAY PRAY PRAY P

EEP KEEP KEEP KEE
ALM CALM CALM CALI
ND AND AND AND
AY PRAY PRAY PRAY

KEEP KEEP KEEP
CALM CALM CALM
AND AND AND
PRAY PRAY PRAY P

KEEP CALM AND PRAY

Disturb us, Lord,
to dare more boldly,
To venture on wider seas
Where storms will show
your mastery;
Where losing sight of land,
We shall find stars.

Francis Drake

Prepare the way of the Lord, make his paths straight.

Matthew 3:3

Truth and Love are wings
that cannot be separated,
for Truth cannot fly without
Love, nor can Love soar
aloft without Truth; their
yoke is one of amity.

Ephrem the Syrian

So if anyone is in Christ, there is a new creation: everything old has passed away; see, everything has become new!

2 Corinthians 5:17

We are not human beings having a spiritual experience; we are spiritual beings having a human experience.

Pierre Teilhard de Chardin

*For it was you who
formed my inward parts;
you knit me together in
my mother's womb.
I praise you, for
I am fearfully and
wonderfully made.*

Psalm 139:13–14

Your hand
upholds the universe,
Your love gives rest
to the world.

Cyrillona

See, I am sending you
out like sheep into the
midst of wolves; so be wise
as serpents and innocent
as doves.

Matthew 10:16

Thank God every morning, when you get up, that you have something to do that day which must be done, whether you like it or not.

Charles Kingsley

Our salvation is in loving and cherishing his creation, in so living that others may have life.

Gerard W. Hughes

Most merciful Redeemer,
Friend and Brother,
may we know you
more clearly,
love you more dearly,
and follow you more nearly,
day by day.

Richard of Chichester

Endeavour seven times a day to withdraw from business and company and lift up thy soul to God in private retirement.

Adoniram Judson

The lark's on the wing;
The snail's on the thorn;
God's in His heaven –
All's right with the world!

Robert Browning

… and what does the Lord require of you but to do justice, and to love kindness, and to walk humbly with your God?

Micah 6:8

O God, to those who have hunger, give bread, and to us who have bread, give the hunger for justice.

Latin American prayer

I worry until midnight
and from then on I let
God worry.

Luigi Guanella

God is our refuge and
strength, a very present
help in trouble.

Psalm 46:1

The glory of
Christianity is
to conquer by
forgiveness.

William Blake

Forgiving is not forgetting;
it's actually remembering –
remembering and not using
your right to hit back.

Desmond Tutu

*Teach us, good Lord,
to serve you as you
deserve, to give and not
to count the cost...
save that of knowing
that we do your will.*

Ignatius of Loyola

When he tells us
to love our enemies,
He gives, along with
the command, the
love itself.

Corrie ten Boom

Blessed are the merciful,
for they will receive mercy.
Blessed are the pure in
heart, for they will see God.

Matthew 5:7–8

No pain, no palm;
no thorn, no throne…

William Penn

Breathe on me,
Breath of God,
Fill me with life anew,
That I may love what
thou dost love,
And do what thou
wouldst do.

Edwin Hatch

The darker the night,
the brighter the stars,
The deeper the grief,
the closer is God!

Fyodor Dostoyevsky

When we are nothing,
we are in a fine
position to receive
everything from God.

Richard Rohr

… give us the true courage that shows itself in gentleness, the true wisdom that shows itself in simplicity, and the true power that shows itself in modesty.

Charles Kingsley

We are closest to
God in the darkness,
stumbling along
blindly.

Madeleine L'Engle

For most of us the prayer in Gethsemane is the only model. Removing mountains can wait.

C. S. Lewis

The function of prayer is not
to influence God, but rather
to change the nature of the
one who prays.

Søren Kierkegaard

✝

As he went ashore,
he saw a great crowd;
and he had compassion
for them, because they
were like sheep without a
shepherd; and he began
to teach them…

Mark 6:34

*God be in my heart,
and in my thinking;
God be at my end,
and at my departing.*

The Sarum Primer

If I speak in the tongues
of mortals and of angels,
but do not have love,
I am a noisy gong or a
clanging cymbal.

1 Corinthians 13:1

God is silent.
Now if only man
would shut up.

Woody Allen

Little children, keep
yourselves from idols.

1 John 5:21

Keep awake and pray
that you may not come into
the time of trial; the spirit
indeed is willing, but the
flesh is weak.

Mark 14:38

No point in becoming
a saint by halves. I'm
not afraid of suffering for
your sake; the only thing
I'm afraid of is clinging to
my own will.

Thérèse of Lisieux

Be a sinner and sin boldly, but believe and rejoice in Christ even more boldly.

Martin Luther

Whoever does the will
of God is my brother
and sister and mother.

Mark 3:35

Where you go, I will go:
where you lodge,
I will lodge;
your people shall
be my people,
and your God my God.

Ruth 1:16

If you want to make
God laugh, tell him
about your plans.

Woody Allen

All I can 'pay back' to
God or others or myself
is who I really am.

Richard Rohr

Blessed are the poor in
spirit, for theirs is the
kingdom of heaven.
Blessed are those who
mourn, for they will
be comforted.

Matthew 5:3–4

*Your hand has
been over me
and has guarded
and preserved me.*

Dietrich Bonhoeffer

God will not look
you over for medals,
degrees or diplomas
but for scars.

Elbert Hubbard

So we can say
with confidence, 'The Lord
is my helper; I will not be
afraid. What can anyone
do to me?'

Hebrews 13:6

✝

I sought to hear the voice of God and climbed the topmost steeple, but God declared: 'Go down again – I dwell among the people.'

John Henry Newman

Let the night be too
dark for me to see
Into the future.
Let what will be, be.

Robert Frost

Have you believed because
you have seen me?
Blessed are those who
have not seen and yet
have come to believe.

John 20:29

We may be surprised
at the people we find
in heaven. God has a
soft spot for sinners.

Desmond Tutu

*O Lord, help me
not to despise or
oppose what I do
not understand.*

William Penn

God whispers to us in our
pleasures, speaks in our
consciences, but shouts
in our pains.

C. S. Lewis

One shall not kill 'the evil impulse', the passion, in oneself, but one shall serve God with it…

Martin Buber

Open wide the door of our hearts, that we may receive and entertain Thee with all our powers of adoration and love. Amen.

Christina Rossetti

… my flesh is frail and weak. If I therefore at any time forget Thee, touch my heart, O Lord, that I may again remember Thee.

Queen Elizabeth I

Blessed are those who hunger and thirst for righteousness, for they will be filled.

Matthew 5:6

Even though I walk through the darkest valley, I fear no evil; for you are with me; your rod and your staff – they comfort me.

Psalm 23:4

Had Mary been filled
with reason
There'd have been no
room for the child.

Madeleine L'Engle

He became what we
are that he might
make us what he is.

Athanasius of Alexandria

My soul magnifies the Lord,
and my spirit rejoices
in God my Saviour,
for he has looked with
favour on the lowliness
of his servant.

Luke 1:46–48

The Bible without the
Holy Spirit is a sundial
by moonlight.

Dwight L. Moody

Arise, shine; for your light
has come, and the glory of
the Lord has risen upon you.

Isaiah 60:1

*Dear Lord, be good
to me. The sea is so
wide, and my boat
is so small.*

Prayer of an Irish fisherman

God is the only one who
can make the valley of
trouble a door of hope.

Catherine Marshall

Behold, miracle of miracles,
out of the cracks a
light shines.

Choan-Seng Song

You will pray to him,
and he will hear you...

Job 22:27

The most difficult and decisive part of prayer is acquiring this ability to listen. Listening is no passive affair.

Mother Mary Clare SLG

Thou, O Lord, that stillest the raging of the sea, hear, hear us, and save us...

Book of Common Prayer

So begin: and continually
repeat and repeat, but all
the time keep before you the
thought of our Lord.

Theophan the Recluse, on prayer

Just as the eye perceives light and the ear sound, the heart is the organ for meaning.

David Steindl-Rast

Ask, and it will be given you;
search and you will find;
knock, and the door will
be opened for you.

Matthew 7:7

Joy runs deeper
than despair.

Corrie ten Boom

*Oh, God of Dust
and Rainbows,
Help us to see
That without the
dust the rainbow
would not be.*

Langston Hughes

And when it rains on your parade, look up rather than down. Without the rain, there would be no rainbow.

G. K. Chesterton

Darkness cannot
drive out darkness:
only light can do that.
Hate cannot drive out hate:
only love can do that.

Martin Luther King, Jr

If you have never
had any distractions
you don't know
how to pray.

Thomas Merton

If you plan to build a
high house of virtues,
you must first lay deep
foundations of humility.

Augustine of Hippo

Prayer is nothing else
than being on terms of
friendship with God.

Teresa of Ávila

Pray as you can, and do not try to pray as you can't.

John Chapman

… let me see thee face to face… thou dearest Jesus, whom my soul longeth after.

William Romaine

God sends no one
away empty except
those who are full of
themselves.

Dwight L. Moody

It is a splendid habit to laugh inwardly at yourself. It is the best way of regaining your good humour and of finding God without further anxiety.

Henri de Tourville

There is no limit
that can be set to
our growth in our
Godward life, since
the good has
no limit…

Gregory of Nyssa

Whatever else I am
dissatisfied with, there is
one whom I can contemplate
with utter satisfaction and
bathe my stained soul in
that eternal fount of purity.

Charles Kingsley

They who have all that they
want and desire, know joy.
But no one has this except
those whose will is one
with God's will.

Meister Eckhart

I will thank him for
the pleasures given
me through my
senses, for the glory
of the thunder, for the
mystery of music...

Edward King

*Grant me, O Lord,
a sunny mind…*

Emily Dickinson

For it is certain that
whatever seeming calamity
happens to you, if you thank
and praise God for it, you
turn it into a blessing.

William Law

… the Lord gave, and the Lord has taken away; blessed be the name of the Lord.

Job 1:21

The tears of our own grief
can soften our hardened
hearts and open us to the
possibility to say 'thanks'.

Henri Nouwen

I shall revive at thy light; my vital spirits will confess thy presence. Grief and anxiety will vanish before thee, and immortal joys surround my soul.

Elizabeth Rowe

You can do very little
with faith, but you can
do nothing without it.

Samuel Butler

Human beings must
be known to be loved,
but divine things must
be loved to be known.

Blaise Pascal

Understanding is the reward of faith. Therefore, seek not to understand that thou mayest believe, but believe that thou mayest understand.

Augustine of Hippo

… in prosperity prayers
seem but a mere medley
of words, until misfortune
comes and the unhappy
sufferer first understands
the meaning of the sublime
language…

Alexandre Dumas

I've read the last page of the Bible. It's all going to turn out all right.

Billy Graham

Be still, and know that I am God!

Psalm 46:10

The fear of the Lord is
the beginning of knowledge;
fools despise wisdom
and instruction.

Proverbs 1:7

It is perfectly evident to my mind that there exists a necessary, eternal, supreme, and intelligent being. This is no matter of faith, but of reason.

Voltaire

*My spirit longs
for thee,
Within my
troubled breast,
Though I unworthy be
Of so divine a guest.*

John Byrom

God instructs the heart
not by ideas, but by pains
and contradictions.

Jean Pierre de Caussade

When He plans
to plant a garden,
He starts in the desert.

Patricia St. John

*Teach me, O God…
to breathe deeply
in faith.*

Søren Kierkegaard

Make sure you are
doing what God wants
you to do – then do it
with all your strength.

George Washington

No man can be
called friendless who
has God and the
companionship of
good books.

Elizabeth Barrett Browning

*As the first Adam's
sweat surrounds my face,
May the last Adam's blood
my soul embrace.*

John Donne

O Jesus, I have promised
To serve thee to the end;
Be thou for ever near me,
My Master and my Friend...

John E. Bode

Let us take things as we find them: let us not attempt to distort them into what they are not... We cannot make facts... We must use them.

John Henry Newman

… it is in the unclouded night-sky, where His worlds wheel their silent course, that we read clearest His infinitude, His omnipotence, His omnipresence.

Charlotte Brontë

If God were not willing
to forgive sin, heaven
would be empty.

German proverb

Lord Jesus Christ,
Son of God,
have mercy on me,
a sinner.

The Jesus Prayer

Eternity is not something that begins after you are dead. It is going on all the time. We are in it now.

Charlotte Perkins Gilman

God loves each of us
as if there were only
one of us.

Augustine of Hippo

It is easier to know God than
our own soul, for God is
nearer than that…

Julian of Norwich

Earth's crammed
with heaven,
And every common bush
afire with God,
But only he who sees,
takes off his shoes,
The rest sit round it and
pluck blackberries...

Elizabeth Barrett Browning

Alone with none
but thee, my God,
I journey on my way.
What need I fear when
thou art near
O king of night
and day?

Columba

Come down, O love divine,
Seek thou this soul of mine,
And visit it with thine own
ardour glowing...

Bianco da Siena

By perseverance the snail reached the ark.

Charles Spurgeon

Stupidity is also a
gift of God, but one
mustn't misuse it.

Pope John Paul II

I would rather say five words devoutly with my heart, than five thousand which my soul does not relish with affection and understanding.

Edmund the Martyr

What I kept, I lost.
What I spent, I had.
What I gave, I have.

Persian proverb

✝

But when we speak
with God, our power of
addressing Him…
and listening to His still
small voice, depends
on our will being one and
the same with His.

Florence Nightingale

One grain of love
is better than a
hundredweight
of intellect.

Edward Bouverie Pusey

The capital of heaven is
the heart in which Jesus is
enthroned as King.

Sadhu Sundar Singh

*Forth in thy Name,
O Lord, I go, my daily labour
to pursue; Thee, only thee,
resolved to know in all I
think or speak or do.*

Charles Wesley

We can only know God well by knowing our iniquities. Therefore those who have known God, without knowing their wretchedness, have not glorified Him, but have glorified themselves.

Blaise Pascal

For everything there
is a season, and a
time for every matter
under heaven...

Ecclesiastes 3:1

O Lord, Thou knowest how busy I must be this day. If I forget Thee, do not forget me.

Jacob Astley, 1st Baron Astley of Reading (before going into battle)

Take heart, daughter;
your faith has
made you well.

Matthew 9:22

I have formerly lived
by hearsay and faith; but
now I go where I shall live
by sight, and shall be with
him in whose company
I delight myself.

John Bunyan

*Lord, make me an
instrument of your peace.
Where there is hatred,
let me sow love…
Where there
is darkness, light,
And where there
is sadness, joy.*

Francis of Assisi

Keep your lives
free from the love
of money, and be
content with what you
have; for he has said,
'I will never leave you
or forsake you.'

Hebrews 13:5

*Bestow upon me, O Lord
my God, an understanding
that knows thee, wisdom
in finding thee… and
confidence that I shall
embrace thee at the last.*

Thomas Aquinas

I will sing to my God
a new song: O Lord,
you are great and
glorious, wonderful in
strength, invincible.

Judith 16:13

For I am convinced
that neither death, nor life…
nor things present, nor
things to come… will be
able to separate us from
the love of God…

Romans 8:38–39

Faith is the highest passion in a human being. Many in every generation may not come that far, but none comes further.

Søren Kierkegaard

In the midst of winter,
I found there was within me,
an invincible summer.

Albert Camus

When the solution
is simple, God is
answering.

Albert Einstein

Grace is love that cares
and stoops and rescues.

John Stott

O thou lord of life,
send my roots rain.

Gerard Manley Hopkins

*Give me my
scallop-shell of quiet,
My staff of faith to
walk upon…
My gown of glory,
hope's true gage,
And thus I'll take my
pilgrimage.*

Walter Raleigh

I fear God, yet I am not afraid of him.

Thomas Browne

In returning and rest
you shall be saved; in
quietness and in trust
shall be your strength.

Isaiah 30:15

For now we see in a mirror, dimly, but then we will see face to face. Now I know only in part; then I will know fully…

1 Corinthians 13:12

If I am in sickness, my sickness may serve Him; in perplexity, my perplexity may serve Him; if I am in sorrow, my sorrow may serve Him.

John Henry Newman

Grace be with all
who have an undying
love for our Lord
Jesus Christ.

Ephesians 6:24

Faith is awe in the
presence of the divine
incognito…

Karl Barth

All shall be well, and all shall be well, and all manner of thing shall be well.

Julian of Norwich

The world thirsts for
grace. When grace
descends, the world
falls silent before it.

Philip Yancey

Tension, anxiety,
worry, frustration, all melt
away before him, as snow
before the sun.

Jim Borst

Always he is with us.
And, in the long run,
that is all we need
to know.

David Watson

*May He support us all day
long, till the shades lengthen
and the evening comes, and
the busy world is hushed,
and the fever of life is over.*

John Henry Newman

And now faith, hope, and
love abide, these three; and
the greatest of these
is love.

1 Corinthians 13:13

I am the Alpha and the
Omega, the first and
the last, the beginning
and the end.

Revelation 22:13

If you're interested in finding out more about our books, find us on Facebook at **Summersdale Publishers** and follow us on Twitter at **@Summersdale**

www.summersdale.com

KEEP KEEP KEEP KE
CALM CALM CALM CA
AND AND AND AN
PRAY PRAY PRAY PRA

EP KEEP KEEP KEEP
LM CALM CALM CALM
AND AND AND
Y PRAY PRAY PRAY

KEEP KEEP KEEP KE
CALM CALM CALM CA
AND AND AND AN
PRAY PRAY PRAY PRA

EP KEEP KEEP KEEP
LM CALM CALM CALM
AND AND AND
Y PRAY PRAY PRAY

KEEP CALM AND PRAY